To those who see
     bare branches –
and know they hold the buds of spring

to those who see
     stars falling in the heavens –
     and know the constellations will remain forever

          to those who see
               long lines of geese
                    fade far beyond –
          and know they come back again to nest

          to those who see
               with wonder in their hearts –
          and know – what glories there can be

               for those who see . . . . . .

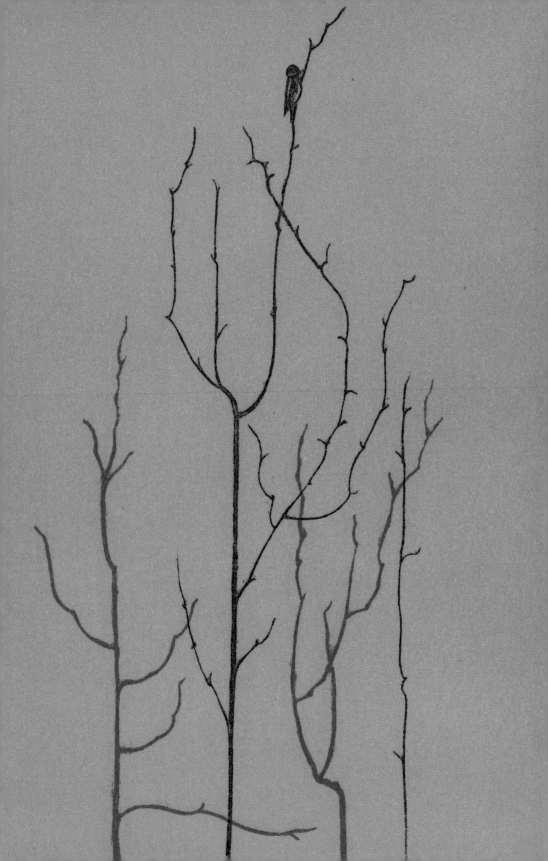

To Those Who See

. . . Gwen Frostic

The wildness calls —
and in the snow
are tracks that lead us on - - - - -

the winds blow freshness to our lives
and stars seem
close enough to touch . . . . . .

Intensely they live
    each hour of the day
In purposeful waiting
    and purposeful flight - - - - -

    They burst into song
        or soar with the winds
    A deep sense of urgency
        prevails through their lives . . . .

They have their limitations - - as all things do - - - - -
yet they live so fully within their sphere that birds shall
        ever seem to be - - - - -
                wild - - - -
                    beautiful - - - -
                        and free . . . ., ...

The keenness of their eyes gives them vision to spot the
tiniest bit of food - - and with alacrity and precision of
motion they pick it up . . . . . .   Theirs is a world of
instant decisions and quick action . . . . . .

They know each wind - - - - -   the sound of rain - -
        the beauty of their own soft feathers . . . . .
They know the sun - - - - the starry nights - - -
        and clouds that ever come and go . . . .

They sing songs without words - - - - - knowing that
somewhere there is a mate that understands - - -
  - a low clear call in the night
    - - a joyful melody at dawn
      - - - or a vesper lyric at sundown
love songs thrown to the sky carried by the winds . . . .
And so they mate - - - - and build their homes and
while the young ones chirp - - they feed them well and
show each one the wondrous way of birds - - for soon
the young will leave the nest to sing their own songs -
- - - find their own food - - - - and know the freedom
of independence . . . .

They may pass from time to time - - - - - and travel
together across the miles - - - each to himself - - - -
yet - - - bound by common ways . . . .

      When the south wind begins to blow - -
          and the earth turns green with life - - -
      Love springs anew - - - -
          and the ancient songs are heard again
          Songs of the
              wild - - -
              the beautiful - - - -
                  and free . . . .

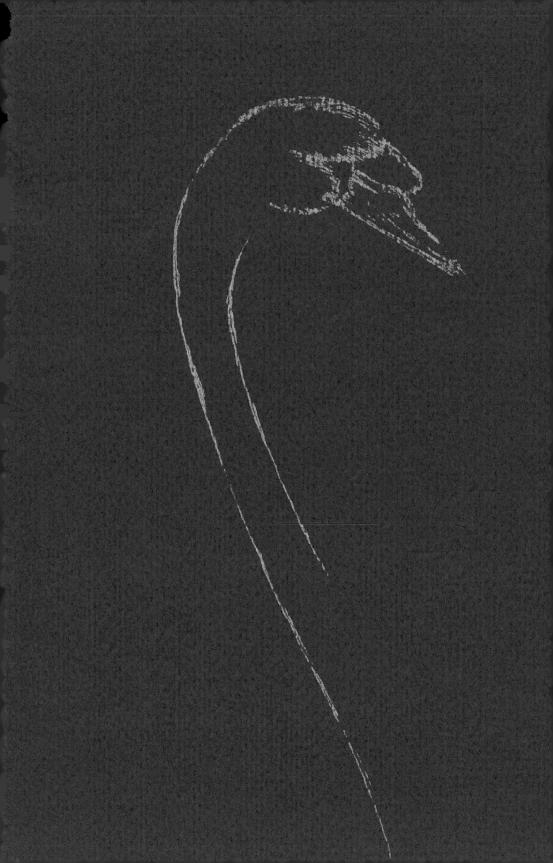

Within the circularity of it all – – –
    the cosmic riddle of
        life - - and death -
                - - and life – again

    Each swan is always a swan - - -
          with all its beauty and grace

    and - - - the blue jay remains a jay – –

    No turtle would try to induce
        a frog - to live his way . . . .

Perhaps . . . .
    there-in – –
      lies the secret
        of peaceful coexistence . . . .

- - - - yellowed leaves floating in the air
              bare stalks stand erect
      holding next year's pussy willows to the sky

thus - - - -
          there is no beginning - - and no ending - - - -
              - - only a slow blending - - -
      day into night - - - fall into winter into spring - - -

beauty - - - - -
          to the eye that beholds it
                  is the one consistency . . . . . .

In the cathedral of the woods
        where the slanting light shines through

The song of a bird enchants the air
        and fills the soul with tranquillity . .

        Over the open fields the spirit glides
            on the wing of a bee - - - -
                            or a dragonfly
            touching each flower growing there - - - - -

and - - as the day slips into night
        finds beauty in a blade of grass . . . .

Slowly the great panorama of color changes into purples and greys - - - - -

day is becoming night . . . . . .
Trees stand silhouetted against subdued light - - - - - - life of the day is quietly resting as the vigilant life of night is stirring . . . .

The evening star glistens beside the pale crescent of the new moon which seems to pause a moment on the horizon - - then slips beyond . . . .

Thousands of fireflies twinkle in the low fields - - - twinkling to their mates - - - - then rise in ecstasy and mingle with the stars . . . . . .

Stars that reach down and touch the waters of the pool on still nights - - - - and make new fallen snow sparkle with reflected light . . . . . . Milliards of stars form a great arc across the heavens and create a luminous light . . There are summer nights when stars shoot out of the darkness and almost drop to earth . . . .

Even among the steadfast stars
there is change and motion . . . .
There are nights when the northern sky becomes a shimmering curtain with vertical rays of greens - - - yellows - - and shades of rose - - - moving - - - moving - - - constantly changing . . . .

- - - nights of reverence
        and tranquil solitude - - - -
time for the imagination to recreate itself . . . . . .

Nights when the full moon rises - - - a huge
orange ball of reflected light - - - - clouds move
swiftly over it as the winds form them into ever
changing creations of light and air . . . .

Nights when a great light flashes - - - trees
sway and leaves fly from their branches - - with
each flash the earth is bright - - then rains come
- - - and after the rains - - - - - calm . . . . . .

Only to the eyes of day
              does night seem dark . . . . .
To the moth that follows the fragrance
              of the night-blooming flowers - - -
to the birds that fly
              the migration ways by night - - - -
     to the possums - - - and beavers - - -
          the frogs that trill - - - - -
          and the countless insects
     that lift their wings into the summer dusk - -

night is life - - - - - -
          as beautiful and wondrous - - - - -
              as adventurous and daring - - -
                    as life in the sun . . . . .

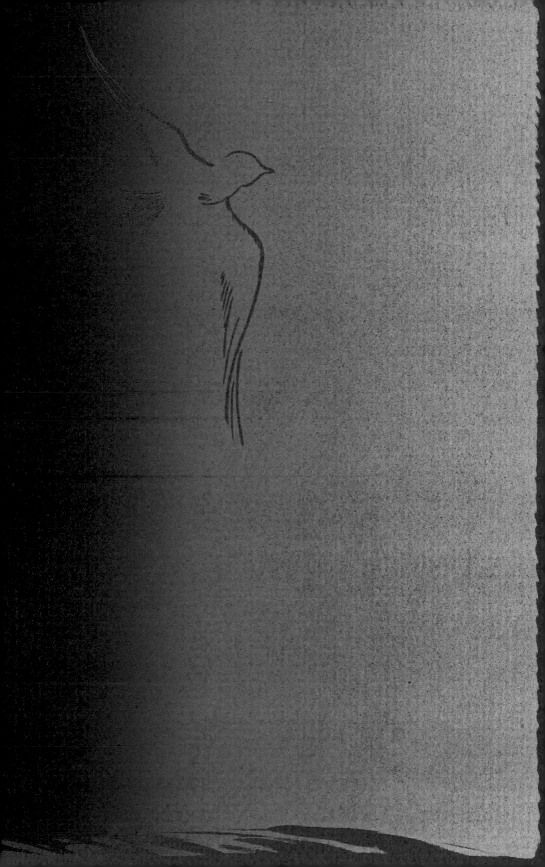

As the far horizons begin to glow - - -
the whip-poor-will circles his world once
more and settles for his rest - - - - -

the morning star is bright - - - - -
slowly the light comes again - - - - - and
a new day has dawned - - - - - - - - - -

Winds and cold days - - -
warm sunlight and running sap - - -
chilly nights - - - then cold again - - - -
between these fluctuations the vernal spirit is steadily
transforming the earth from its cold sleep into its era of
expectation and fulfilment . . . .

Snow is melting - - making little rivers run into
still pools - - - - - the air is warm - - as cedars begin
to show the fresh green of renewed life . . . . . .

The sun is setting slightly farther toward the north . .

In the night a sharp wind brings new snow - - -
the day is dark with clouds - - - birds fluff their feathers
and face the wind . . . . . .

. . . . but the sun is rising a little earlier and going
down a little later - - - each day . . . . .

Pussy willows are silvery greys - - osier - intense
reds - - - - - the long golden twigs of the willows are
swaying - - - omens of things to come . . . .

As the sun makes each day a little longer - - - -
each night a little shorter . . . .

The fuzzy leaves of the mullein are uncurling where last year's stalks stood tall . . . Lichens glow on the trunks of trees - - - - crows call to each other as they arrive in small groups . . . .

The cold strikes again - - - - tiny icicles of sap hang from the branches of the pines - - the beech is glistening in ice . . . .

The morning sun turns the hillside golden - - - - - and through the day its rays are more direct - - - a flock of wild geese is silhouetted in the twilight - - - - -

- - - the day will dawn earlier tomorrow . . . . .

The tops of the birches are red and the hills beyond are delicate greys - - greens - - - - and shades of rose - - - - the buds of the trees are beginning to swell . . . .

Once more the air turns cold - - - golden eyes coming in for a landing skid across the clear ice of the pond - - - a spider skips over the snow - - and red-wings hail the day . . . . . .

Through it all - - - - the earth is continuously being warmed by the sun - - - - and from that warmth - skunk cabbage pushes up - - as each day breaks earlier and dusk comes a little later . . .

The morning snow falls fast and heavy - - - birds find shelter in the swampland - - - - - and wait - - - for now - it cannot last . . . . .

Now - - - - life in all its countless forms is beginning to stir - - - timed to the cycle of the sun - - - each life is born on time . . . .

Eggs of turtles - - - frogs - - and insects are hatching - - - millions of seeds are sprouting - - - - - the things which will not awaken are giving life to those that do - - - - - and thereby shall live again this spring - - - and always . . . . . .

The sun is higher - - - - the days are longer - - - and the magic of spring has touched every living thing - - - each - attuned to life - - - is ready to rise in a mystical kinship with beauty . . .

It's the time of tiny leaves - - - - - delicate blossoms - - - - and long graceful catkins - - - - the time of fragile hues - - - gentle rains - - - and the glowing days that sunshine brings - - - - -

Each leaf in the woods now testifies to the renaissance of life - - - there is music in the air - - - - and intense activity - - - - - - -

The light - - earth - and waters have brought forth new life - - - - - - life with all its freedom - - - its deep mysteries - - - and joyousness - - - - to be lived to the fullest - - - - - where the hunted is also the hunter - - - - each - with its place on earth - - - - - - -

- - - - - and the days go on - - - in never changing pace - - - each a little longer - - - - - each night a little shorter - - - - - until that time when earth turns back again - - - - -

- - - - toward winter - - - - - -

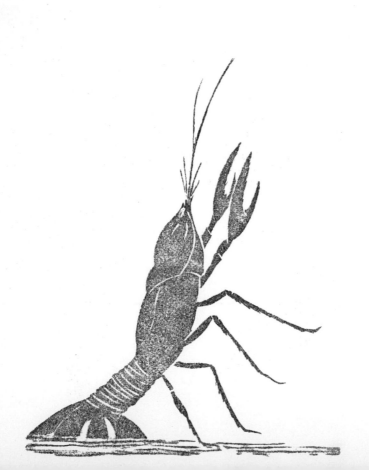

Each life is precious - -

                        unto itself −
from the tiniest insect
            to the greatest tree . . . . .
Vigorously it must protect
      its right to be - -
    - - - and to become . . . . .

Upon this one obsession
    rests ~ ~ ~ ~
    the continuance of the universe . . .

Along a path where gentians grow
are some in deepest blue - - - -
some in purest white - - - -
and all the shades between . . . .
Some have many tiers of flowers - -
- - - some have only one . . .
Yet each one is - - - -
and shall remain
a gentian - - - dark or light . . . . .

The weather-beaten jack pine of the dunes
will spread its limbs
and hold its green crown high - - -
when growing in a sheltered spot . . . . . .
Whatever winds may shape its life - - - - -
the soil - - the rains - - - the sun - - - -
It still retains - - - - - and ever shall - -
the characteristics of its kind . . .

caterpillar - - -

cocoon - - -

butterfly -

can one not believe in miracles . . . . . ?

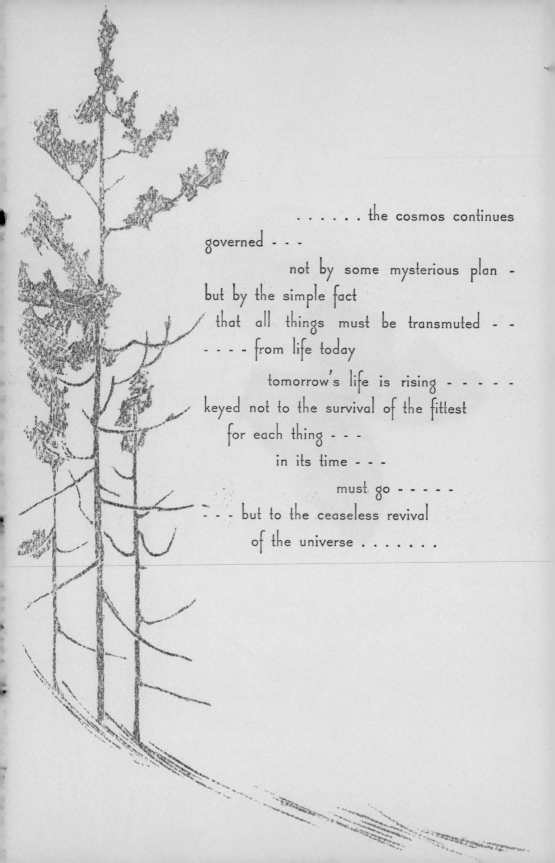

. . . . . . the cosmos continues

governed - - -

not by some mysterious plan -
but by the simple fact
that all things must be transmuted - -
- - - - from life today

tomorrow's life is rising - - - - -
keyed not to the survival of the fittest
for each thing - - -

in its time - - -

must go - - - - -
- - - but to the ceaseless revival
of the universe . . . .

A great majestic heron stands - - -

- - - waiting - - - -

soon - a little green frog

will become part of a bird

that will fly to great heights in the sky - - - - - - -

- - - yet - - - - there will always be - - -

little green frogs - - - - -

to trill in the ponds of spring . . . . . .

- - - to those who see
        miraculous sights
            and envision all of the wonders
                hidden from the eye - - - -

        hear multitudinous sounds
            and listen to the symphonies
                that silence brings . . . . . .